Wakefield Press

MIDWINTER LIGHT

Born in 1933, Ann Timoney Jenkin grew up in wartime London. She has lived in Adelaide since 1960. Her poetry and short stories have been widely published in anthologies and magazines and are broadcast on the ABC. She writes children's stories, is a professional storyteller, regularly gives poetry workshops and has worked as an editor. This is her first collection of poetry.

MIDWINTER

LIGHT

Poems by

ANN TIMONEY JENKIN

Wakefield Press

Wakefield Press
Box 2266
Kent Town
South Australia 5071

First Published 1995

Text designed and typeset by Tabloid Pty Ltd, Adelaide
Cover designed by Kerry Argent, Adelaide
Printed and bound by Hyde Park Press, Adelaide

ISBN 1 86254 365 8

Promotion of this book was assisted by the
Commonwealth Government through the Australia Council,
its arts funding and advisory body.

To my father
James Alexander Timoney
1899-1975

'human kind
Cannot bear very much reality.'

ACKNOWLEDGEMENTS

Most of the poems in this collection have been
previously published and acknowledgement is made to
the *Adelaide Review*, the *Bulletin, Island Magazine,
Opinion, Poetry Australia* and *Quadrant*.

Poems have appeared in the following anthologies:
Friendly Street Readers – Nos. 7-18, *The Inner Courtyard,
Patterson Literary Review '92* and *'94* (USA),
Arrival Press Spring Collection '93 (UK) and *Tuesday Night Live*.

The sequence of eight, *Poems for My Father*, was published in
The Sea's White Edge, the Mattara Prize Winner's Anthology
edited by Paul Kavanagh and published by Butterfly Press.

Six of the poems in this Collection appeared in *Hope and Fear:
An Anthology of S.A. Women's Writing*, published in 1994
to commemorate the centenary of women's suffrage.

Many poems have been broadcast on 5RN and 5CK
(ABC Radio), and also on Radio 5UV.

I would like to thank the South Australian Department of Arts
and Cultural Heritage for financial assistance. An Individual
Project Grant assisted me in the production of this manuscript.

CONTENTS

Poems for my Father

Pruning Roses 3

Easter Morning 4

Shadows from the War 5

Bombed Out 6

Cherry Tree 7

Between the Lines 8

1 March 1975 9

London Re-Visited 10

Travelling East

Barossa Heights 13

Threshold 14

Ash Wednesday 15

A Time of Change 17

Sonnet 18

Quadrina for the First Day of Winter 19

Winter Solstice 20

Do Not Stand Too Close 21

The Mind's Way 22

Dubbo Bus Terminus 23

Travelling East 25

Quadrina for a Wedding 26

The Punch and Judy Man 27

Migrant Women

Night Train 31

Migrant Women 32

Postcard from Lyon 33

Chicory Coffee 34

A Cornish Cemetery 35

A Nice Drop of Rain 37

After the Divorce 38

Christmas Shopping 39

After the Wedding 40

Pantoum: On Turning 60 41

Diamond Wedding 42

After the Wake 43

Wind Bells

Furnished Rooms 47

Wind Bells 48

Three Grandmothers 49

Jacaranda Days 51

Cancer Care 53

Poem for the End 54

Poems for my Father

Pruning Roses

My father always pruned the roses
ritually, showed me how to find
the outside bud, to trim and shape
and yet allow the plant to breathe and grow.
We'd burn the prunings – green sap
spat and hissed. I breathed
the wood smoke in for life
to mingle with my breath
on winter days.
I never can quite cut them
down to size. Those winter hips,
bright bitter lanterns
travelling through the years.
Midwinter light stands still.

Easter Morning

Did you see the sun dance then?
My father always asked.
I never did, would sleepy smile and sigh.
His early morning cigarette
puffing out his thoughts like prayers
his paschal smile a secret place.
Enamelled kettle singing hymns
for strong sweet tea
we'd sip and share
still sleeping household silent.
Our quiet communion breathing thoughts
for me to travel by
and find in Lenten years
a dancing sun.

Shadows from the War

LONDON 1940

To stop me counting bombs
you showed me how a light could fall
and move and change the way things seem.
Made shadow puppets on the wall
your hand a tall giraffe
that stalked across the world
in our small room.
Snug blackout tight and trim
enclosed our light within.

* * *

I watch winter sun dapple
with the gentleness a longer distance brings.
Watch it walk down the wall
brick by brick
towards the spring.

Bombed Out

JUNE 1944

The night our house was bombed
I missed the whole damned thing:
a child asleep.
Dreamed swirling debris, dust and wind –
the skeetering of glass across a cage.
My mother's fear snapped me awake
softly calling: 'Jimmy, are you there?'
That night you would not leave your book
your innerworld affair.
We crept through dusty darkness,
tiptoed over bits of ceilings
fallen doors and scrunchy glass
the stricken house still creaking from its wounds
and searched for you.

And there
your old armchair
upturned and spiky now with shafts of glass
glinting in the torchlight.
Your old armchair so slowly moved and you
emerged – torpid, turtle-like, unscathed
and dazed, still clutching 'Mansfield Park'.
We hardly dared to breathe
while you flowed in the fearful space
that emptied out of us.
Four pairs of eyes acknowledged that
our family was still alive.
And then the cat appeared
and we all cheered.

Cherry Tree

LONDON 1947

All those growing years it flowered
outside my bedroom window.
A rosy filter for the morning lens,
survivor of the war.
One year it snowed in May,
white confetti gently clung:
a lethal quilting down.
Full blossomed branches on the rack
to crack at last in death.
You watched in utter quiet
while I discovered grief
and learned to mourn the end of things
lost in the rites of snow
that frozen spring.

Between the Lines

Twenty years of letters from abroad
telling life as we would have it be:
I wrote of children, holidays and treats,
told funny stories of our migrant lives
and entertained you with my flair for fiction;
your witty letters thanking God
for female correspondence, memories and me.
I always read you first between the lines –
our cryptic code, our understated way.
Behind forgotten convent walls a stifled girl
still dreamed a life that could not be.
Perhaps you knew. Sometimes I glimpsed
your sadness underneath. You wrote 'The Gods
give nuts to those that have no teeth.'

1 March 1975

They told me you stopped breathing in the street –
to die alone in such a public place?
The telephone at three a.m. said 'peacefully'.
I sat alone, cocoon-like in a blanket
a contemplating crone that summer night
to wait in every moment wide awake
my wake for you.
As walls grew painful round an empty space
I kept through all the years
I searched for you,
insistent morning slithered under doors and windows
that first day you could not be.
The grandchildren you never knew
were sad for me.

London Re-Visited 1975

Back in London no one spoke of you.
I smelt your cigarettes, my head so full
of things to tell I almost saw you – everywhere.
My mother's memory seems tidy clean
all trace of you erased
your clothes your books – those cherished
Austens, Shakespeare, gone all gone
in some long gone church sale.
While on your grave, green glass glinted,
artificial flowers mocked your mortality.

I make our early morning tea
no longer sweet to draw for me.
Then lay fresh roses on your grave
to die goodbye from me.

Travelling East

Barossa Heights

Darkening hills observe
the sun-lit valley. From scrubby gorse
a scolding scrub wren chitters at the stranger's nerve.
The summer storm divines a water course
an easy parting down this giant's thatch. Sheep stare
at the woman with tangled thoughts in her hair –
back to the wind. The sheep say: Follow me.
Their narrow trail winds up the hill to an old gum tree
where fallen branches arch a cave.
The wind's womb, squalling rain's reprieve
and sudden silence say: Be brave
take all the time you need then leave.
The woman strides to the wind. Sheep stare.
And a rising kestrel dances on air.

Threshold

Time ticks. The setting of
our metronome unknown.
And when it stops: the pre-wound
spring undone, the momentary pause
before we go is long enough
to see how much
we managed to become.

I've seen Hell in a dying man
his eyes in that last moment
saw the life he could have lived
if he had known
which chronicle of time
was his alone.

Ash Wednesday

Early morning. Grey slate
now pink – my kitchen floor
reflecting stained glass light:
half window in the door

leads me outside. Late roses
open slowly; take their time
but smell as sweet,
and no one minds

an ancient stem of roses.
Late summer brings the early morning close
as I remember other doors that never opened.
Blackbird sings

then scolds the sleepy cat still blinking
blearily through cobwebs caught across her face.
She doesn't care, her confident slow saunter
lets the whole world know she owns this place.

Still air and scent of artificial rain
remind me of those rain-washed days
when gardens grow: a sprinkler system
just keeps them alive. Our natural ways go deeper.

Hot days my body sweats
inside an air-conditioned house. The full moon
still finds tides behind my darkened windows.
Memories long gone are still in tune

as seasons come and go. Will we
control the world one day – how fast it spins
and how close to the sun? Will wars
break out about whose turn it is to have

an early spring? Bulbs hidden
in dark cupboards know the time to grow.
Easter lilies flower around Ash Wednesday
soft pink trumpets bring to mind

the time when fire left blackened earth behind
but still they grew.
Perhaps we must endure these times.
A thistle in a concrete crack

is not afraid to show the world
we can begin again.
Lent hangs about to greet
the few who still remember

ashes come before a resurrection.
Dark times consume.
The Old World stands aside to see
who mimes the video game this time.

Then watches children play with toys
invented to destroy themselves.
Who smiles at our mock concern –
a ploy which helps us to deny

that war cannot make peace;
the pages torn as Yeats' rough beast
its hour come round at last
slouches towards Bethlehem to be born?

Late afternoon. Harsh sun bleaches
colour from the grinning garden gnome.
I close the door
to keep too much from coming here inside.

A Time of Change

Summer drains the life that we intend.
Bright light has no pity
for the byways
and the corners we would hide.
Gadflies in the mind remember
promises we did not keep.
Night is not long enough for sleeping,
new growth feels too tender.

Autumn is more gentle.
A harvest moon encourages
those quickenings we keep inside.
On windy days when kites fly high
those gadflies hide
behind a cheerful fire.
As nights grow longer there is time
to live this afternoon.

Sonnet

First autumn rain has darkened and defined the day,
re-touched the ancient photo summer bleached;
the path along the creek still finds the way
alone – content the journey's end is out of reach.
Run-off dawdles down the dried up bed
to count the silent stones it left behind,
free-wheeling as the way that lies ahead
becomes the only choice there is to find.
In such a place a thought will quietly grow,
become an utter presence from some source,
as round and round the field awareness flows
to find the still point which becomes the force.
But always words come dropping in the mind
to limit and imprison what's defined.

A Quadrina for the First Day of Winter

Sunshafted garden dripping with late autumn
considered trying on a winter mask
in chilly air, but some late blooming rose
in pink postponed that season's way.

Light falls longer on its way
to shorter days. Reluctant autumn
hangs about like bedtime's child. With mask
in either hand the garden smells its rose.

But fretful now for winter sleep, the rose
throws petals round the garden's way
as winter coldly creeps through autumn
leaves, and slyly fits the drowsy garden's mask.

For who can change the time of winter's mask
when seasons chime, it's time? The sleeping rose
now snug in bed lets winter have its way.
The garden, naked now, has quite forgotten autumn.

Winter Solstice

Each year the light finds unexpected ways
and warms new corners where the cat will sleep
as dead leaves settle for the winter.
Trees have grown or died
or were removed and shadows stretch
along the wall.
On black cloud days
when winter violets wait and watch
the sun still moves
towards the journey's end.
Then light stands still
and shadows hold their breath
to think about a life that's in the sun
or has eternal silence just begun?

Do Not Stand Too Close

Do not stand too close.
My voice becomes an echo then
of someone else's life.
And where's the truth in that
for me I ask?

Do not stand too close.
I cannot feel the wind
or sense a changing mood.
With such lucidity I see
each moment when alone.

When you are too close
I am not brave enough
to be afraid.
And I might try to lean
on your shadow.

The Mind's Way

The night has gathered quietly around
as I read words which started as a thought
somewhere beyond the vision
of this solitary life. And suddenly
the silence fills the room, to change a mood
as if the exposition ended in a minor key
and I am caught
inside an anxious sound.

Within that pause, eternity occurs.

Now thoughts prowl down forgotten ways
to find a life still waiting to be made
and filled with promises I did not keep.

I lock the door before I go to sleep
secure the chain – a physical blockade
for shutting in or shutting out these days.
The moon walks through the night and nothing stirs.

Dubbo Bus Terminus 1.30a.m.

A warm night gathers in the travellers:
small children – floppy with fatigue,
propped up in plastic chairs
while frayed mothers rearrange
plastic bags bursting
with familiar lives.

Young women in bright brief clothing:
mops of frizzy hair
gathered high in bundles –
yawn the waiting time away,
chew fingernails, eat chips
and wonder what to do.
The anxious middle-aged in careful crimplene
clutch handbags and worries close,
try not to look alone.

Women travelling at night
from lives we might have led
towards some endless new beginning.
Outside the world seems soaked in sleep.
Inside, my head sighs at release
from day time thought-blitzing torture
of pop music and jolly-driver chat.

At some unknown signal
we gather ourselves
and wander out to the bus.
The driver hurrying through the dark bus bay
checks slicked back hair, sucks in
a too tight belt and rearranges himself
the way men do when they are anxious.
He is late, and pastes his smile back on
to check us over.
On the blessedly silent bus
we set off.

Travelling East

I wake while the bus
rumbles along the road
towards the next day.
Dawn sneaks across dry paddocks –
trees etched along the skyline.
Night has wiped
my glasses clean.

And there – white cockatoos.
This milling crowd
on a dead gum tree
gives screeching call to prayer:
white paper cut-outs
that the Child-God has created
for His outback Christmas tree.

Thumb-nail moon
our Eastern star
insists on the direction.
While the ghost-like whole,
a Cheshire Cat
leads my thoughts on
to breakfast.

Quadrina for a Wedding

Desiring nothing of the afternoon
steeped in the odour of chrysanthemums
he had thrown away his book about the unicorns
and put an end to that old story.

Waiting without thought, echoes of the story
danced through the shadows of the afternoon.
But he only heard the music of chrysanthemums
singing epitaphs for lazy unicorns.

He found her, reading of the unicorns
her breath filled with the odour of chrysanthemums.
Whispers found the echo of their story
she desired only that they share the afternoon.

Vedic wedding and the open afternoon
give direction to the laughing unicorns.
See the fire uniting friends, quiet chrysanthemums
bear witness. Now begin the telling story.

The Punch and Judy Man

A VILLANELLE

The Punch and Judy man just bowed,
His answer always was the same:
There are no pockets in a shroud.

When all the children laughed out loud
Or booed or hissed the villain's game
The Punch and Judy man just bowed.

A thought-fox creeps in with the crowd,
Small change is all there is to claim:
There are no pockets in a shroud.

As children know who disavowed
And see exactly who's to blame
The Punch and Judy man just bowed.

It is enough. I've been allowed
To sniff the wind and feel the rain:
There are no pockets in a shroud.

So children come and laugh out loud
And see right through the villain's game.
The Punch and Judy man just bowed,
There are no pockets in a shroud.

Migrant Women

Night Train

Black night
consumes the racing train.
Blurred wheels conceal
dots and dashes of coded speech.

Clouds hang out in the sky
tell of a moon invisible.
Is there a town nearby
beckoning in this moment?

Telegraph poles:
stark trees bearing orderly fruit
carry whispered conversations
through the static.

Sleepy travellers
suspended between past and future
doze in a present moment
we still inhabit.

Travelling migrants
on that racing train
hold sleeping children
close.

Homeless through that night
the breakfast orange
a gift
as tempting as Euridice's pomegranate.

Migrant Women

Migrant women
grow where they're planted.
Like weeds
we flower in the wrong place.

Migrant women
stitch themselves
into the fabric:
using only colours
which seem to match.
But light finds the shadows
left over bits
itch.

We will grow old in this place
where insistent sun
bleaches the memory
of touchstones.
Yet our children feel at home
and grow impatient
with mothers who need road maps
and are frightened of the dark.

Postcard From Lyon

Cobbled street.
Is that you in the distance
walking towards me with a large black umbrella
hiding your face? Insistent
rain puddles round your feet:
never closer the whole rest of our lives.
Preserved in sepia, an ancient street survives,
a child becomes a stranger.

Do you see the street lamp
high above your head?
This old city slouches through a cold November dusk
as old walls yawn and spread long shadows closer.
Still you tramp
as motionless as footprints set in stone.
Does the coming darkness hide
what you atone for?

Chicory Coffee

It smells of war.
The peppery bitterness
takes me back to London
fifty years ago.
My father's face
sipping the bitter stuff
with such distaste
our wartime coffee brew.
'This healing plant
is good for you'
my friend exclaims
'It tastes good too.'
How can I tell –
it tastes of war as well.

A Cornish Cemetery

In our beginning
we'd arrive in Newlyn – Easter time
a strange pair even then – that foreign girl from London
married to their local lad made good,
but not above himself they'd hope.
Our urban clocks fast ticking
soon to slow
in tidal pool and deep.

We'd visit the long and newly dead.
The local church at Paul
was visible for miles –
a squat church squarely showing off
its cemetery on Sunday afternoon,
armfuls of daffodils trudging up Paul Hill
to greet the dead;
the wind still singing hymns in wires, a constant hum
to find the pitch of long ago.

'How are you my Lover?' Aunt Nan shouts
across our Lily's grave, then answers:
'I'm alright. I got my Joe – he had me
up Pengelly's field last night.' She laughs
and Lily laughs too –
two years dead – still laughing.

Here's never married skinny Auntie May
with tight smile pasted on her face, bird-eyed bright
still pecking over other people's lives
a scavenger for news, her lost intended
buried on the Somme; she loved us then
cooked indigestion into all our meals.

Kind Aunt Elaine with periwinkle eyes
on top of Uncle Henry six feet deep
the closest now they'd ever been
their bleak eternal sandwich.
He'd said a smile would crack her face in half
but then, her baby died while his lived on –
or so we'd heard.

Pop Larkin – here's the awkward one
a surly stubborn man who mourned
determinedly his dead young wife 'til death.
Raised four young sons with apron strings
cemented in the past.
His Greta Roslein far from home
preserved in his perfection
and this stone – inscribed –
the clumsy German: Lieb von ihren Kinder
marked her exile, alien, alone.

Those early years
we'd slip away
to make our babies up behind a Cornish hedge
out of the wind which sang
a different song. And children came
to build the bridge
I couldn't know I needed.
While misty rain would come in with the tide
insisting that the day must end
but we would live forever
until Sunday.

A Nice Drop of Rain

Nice drop of rain we had last night
he said, looking out of the window.
I stood there silent, suitcase in hand.
I'm leaving, I muttered, all time for shouting gone.
I can't bear it any more,
too empty and dry for any more tears.
A good soak was what we needed
our tomatoes will be great this year –
the pumpkins too, he added.
It's the end this time, I said dully.
This time I'm going.
Why don't you join a choir again?
You used to love to sing –
not that you ever sang for me.
No, my voice was mine.
I never sang for you.
I'm leaving, I said.
Oh come on, enough's enough, you've made your point.
I'll wash up tonight
while you put the kids to bed.
Anyway, where would you go
with no money,
Honey?

After the Divorce

He phoned to ask about the dog
and whether we'd unblocked the bog
remembering how the winter rains
never did improve our drains.
He wondered if I'd like some limes
I thought of all those bitter times
not being rapt in limes
declined.

The camellia, was it in bloom?
I had enough to fill a room.
And yes the garden was a mess
but I was happy none the less.

I felt as if it wasn't me
who talked about the walnut tree
the life we'd shared seemed far away
I never thought that I would say –
    that I would find
    such peace of mind.
You'd never think that it was he
who had so wanted to be free.

Christmas Shopping

The evening light is restless
on the business of Christmas.
Steam rises from
warm, muddied pavements;
rain cannot find
the earth to nourish.

Hissing tyres pursue
a ceaseless tread,
the humid air feels lonely.
As the Town Hall clock strikes
we hurry home
with pumpkins.

After the Wedding

Late afternoon sun
warms a corner of the garden
where three grandmothers sit,
tea grown cold
children and grandchildren ignored –

they had long gone into the house.

Three women tell
the story of their lives –
worlds apart. Drawn together
for this moment
of conclusion.

Their story began
before the house was built.
The day of the wedding
is nearly over. The sun sets
on the beginning of things.

Together they go into the house.

Pantoum: On Turning 60

I remember that place and I was happy there:
yearning for things I won't have again.
I trip over the box of lost futures
there in the attic of my brain.

Yearning for things I won't have again
I flick through the days that are gone.
There in the attic of my brain
with no compass bearings, the mind rambles on.

I flick through the days that are gone:
they all live rent free in my brain.
With no compass bearings the mind rambles on
as the round earth rolls yet again.

They all live rent free in my brain;
filling space where a thought might have grown.
As the round earth rolls yet again
through the darkness a quiet undertone.

Filling space where a thought might have grown:
it is time once again for spring cleaning.
Through the darkness a quiet undertone.
The mind sniffs around – busy gleaning.

It is time once again for spring cleaning.
At the limit of language once more:
the mind sniffs around – busy gleaning.
A garbage truck stops at my door.

At the limit of language once more,
I trip over the box of lost futures.
A garbage truck stops at my door…
I remember that place and I was happy there.

Diamond Wedding

4 APRIL 1989

'Is that you Ann?'
Her long distance surprise
answering my sudden impulse
to hear her voice.
Her pleasure soothing my conscience –
an electronically dutiful daughter
care of Telecom.

'Fancy you remembering!'
As if I could forget
the date my mortality
became possible.
Sole survivors are not recognised
half a bond doesn't count
or years of solitude.

'I wish your father was here.'
She remembers her dress, the day,
her bouquet,
and the shoppers smiling –
worry lines smoothing away
just briefly – that Depression day
sixty years ago.

After the Wake

Last year
I brought flowers for your ninetieth birthday
and you smiled as you scolded me,
could scarcely walk with the arthritic hip
you said was only a pulled muscle.
When it gets better you'll visit me
you promised every year.

Last week
around midnight you went to bed.
The crossword puzzle half finished –
newspaper neatly folded by your chair,
spectacles back in their case,
tiny dictionary alongside.
You switched off the light,
and drew back those red velvet curtains
so the neighbours wouldn't know
what time you got up.
All doors closed.

Then you turned back the bedclothes
and started to undress.
Navy blue skirt neatly folded
over the bedroom chair.
Next a soft wool jumper
a lighter blue – your favourite colour
to match your eyes.
(Your sisters called you Dolly.)

Standing there in your underwear
did you feel unwell?
Notice your heart falter,
then remember that bottle of whiskey
I left for you? You never drank.
Somehow, you reached the cocktail cabinet
in the living room and opened the doors
before you fell.

This week
I sorted your clothes
into five green garbage bags.
Rummaged through drawers and cupboards
looking in vain
for something you might have left behind.

Today
at your funeral
we gave you that good send off you always wanted –
a party you didn't have to attend.
I sit on your green velvet settee;
watch summer sun
filter through French windows
and play with the dust
which hovers
above a bowl of roses.
Evening light explores your house
now the doors are open.
I prop them open
so they won't close
and enjoy the warmth.

Wind Bells

Furnished Rooms

First son, you stir under my plastic apron
I wonder if the bread will last the week.
Flex your musical fingers, I hum the Mozart
you will sing before you learn to speak.

In our cold water kitchen, I would stir
the barley soup, then sit and watch the rain.
Winter kept us warm, and as I slept
along the line of chimney pots you came

somewhere out of the silence. Out of space and time
your presence asked: Is this the right address?
After a while, the light just came and went
smoke hung from the roof tops, motionless.

You lie in a makeshift corner of my room
I sold my bicycle to buy your cot.
Where is that child whose days are there?
You must forget, but I cannot.

Where are the years that walked those days
between the dying and the birth.
What is it that survives – who tries
to sing the music we composed?

Wind Bells

Memory had enlarged the rooms
sent the morning sun streaming through
windows always crystal clean.
But where are those bright colours,
cushions matching – a cosiness?
Who has been sitting in my chair;
worn these holes in the carpet?
My children grew up in this house
before the rooms grew smaller.
We listened to the postman
whistling down the days
and wrote letters home
to grandparents forever there.

I wake from a deep sleep
in a room where I have slept
many times before.
The wind bells are silent
and evening shadows spread long fingers
as the birds of loneliness
come home to roost.
My father stands in the doorway
jingling loose change in his pocket,
one eye closed
against curling cigarette smoke –
a half smile:
shall I go with him?

My grandaughter sings in her cot.

Three Grandmothers

Did you look at your new-mother's face in the mirror
to see if the change were visible
the way women do
when they lose their virginity?

After you told me
I looked at your grandmother's wedding photograph
with my Victorian grandmother you never knew:
Great-Grandmama, her long dark skirts still
brushing shiny black-laced shoes,
hands clasped around a handkerchief for sixty years
her plump face almost smiling.
Old when I was born, she lived in
horse and carriage days. Charles Dickens died
when she was four and learning to roll
a wooden hoop along the grimy London gutters.
Toughened on Irish stew and soda bread
her brother the last of the bare-knuckle fighters;
East-End dockers – a tough gene pool.
She lived through two world wars; her first
two babies died, she had six more.
I was her youngest grandchild, softened her
tough skin – she bought me sweets and let me stir
those Christmas puddings
we still prefer.

Your grandmother on her Wedding Day.
Still frets about her veil that slipped,
a hand's touch could have saved
a sixty year long sigh. Her petite figure
so like yours – will your child have
those deep blue eyes and soft white skin?
We'll know next spring.

Jacaranda Days

Blue light. Your favourite colour.
I drive to the nursing home early;
spring is late.
Blazing jacaranda trees
line the street for you
the nursing home's newest resident.

Imprisoned in a bed recently vacated
by the late Mrs. Sorrel, whose name
above your head in bright gold letters
mocks your impotence
in this house of strangers,
the smell of urine overcomes your flowers.

I take you for a furious walk
in a wheelchair up and down corridors
getting lost until we find the garden
and pretend we've run away to a Never-Never land
where cancer and dementia
are banned.

We talk of those old days.
You – a skilled musician bribed
my children then with cakes
and jokes – wove a love of music
through our ordinary lives
your home and you my refuge.

Back to that bed.
I sit and stroke your hand
and when I leave, your smile
begs me to stay.
Outside, a haze of jacaranda blue.
The gardener sweeping, grumbles too.

Cancer Care

She stands by the basin
trying to wash her dementia
out of soiled knickers
stained with the after effects
of radiotherapy.
The taste of vomit
sours her mouth
tenderised by treatment
designed to prolong
the agony.
'I am not me' she smiles.
'I'll tell the nurses
you brought me flowers.'
I wait and watch
and pray for her to die.

Poem for the End

The pain slinks round your belly
like a cat looking for somewhere to sleep.
Black cat
seeks out the warmest, softest,
secret corner of your bowels
then flexes her claws with delight.
Makes dough with your entrails
purring softly
while you silently scream.

Your staring eyes grieve
for life in these last moments.
Time has ticked full circle
round the life that you intended.

Life stretches on
each grey porridge of a day
sees my new old-woman's face
waking to a monotone
my pockets full of dust.

I busy myself, making a neat plaster cast
of inconsequential things.
I've mended the hole in your waistcoat at last
I kept it when they took away your clothes
meaning to wear it round me like your arms
but there's room for you as well.

On this grey winter's day
the soft rain soothes and your ghost smiles
as I pick the last rose
and my thoughts move
to spring planting.

Wakefield Press

Wakefield Press has been publishing good Australian
books for over fifty years. For a catalogue of current
and forthcoming titles, or to add your name
to our mailing list, send your name and address to

Wakefield Press,
Box 2266,
Kent Town, South Australia 5071.

Telephone (08) 362 8800
Facsimile (08) 362 7592

WAKEFIELD
PRESS